PLAYING THE BASS

BOOK ONE

BY CASSIA HARVEY

CHP301

©2016 by C. Harvey Publications All Rights Reserved.

www.charveypublications.com - print books
www.learnstrings.com - PDF downloadable books
www.harveystringarrangements.com - chamber music

1. Remember the A string

Cassia Harvey

2. Remember the A string with Mississippi Hot Dog

Mix it up a little!

©2016 C. Harvey Publications All Rights Reserved.

3. The Double Notes Song

Each note here gets 2 counts!

4. Remember Mary Had a Little Lamb?

5. Remember the Notes on the D string

6. Practicing While Others Play a D major scale

7. Russian Folk Song

8. Theme from Dvorak's Symphony

Wait while the piano plays 8 measures, then go to the beginning and repeat.

9. Finger Training on D and A

10. Exercise for 1812

11. Tchaikovsky's 1812 Overture

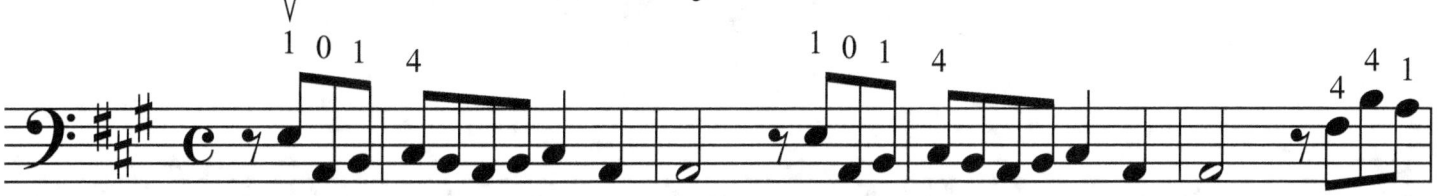

12. *Spring* from Vivaldi's "Four Seasons"

13. Finger Study

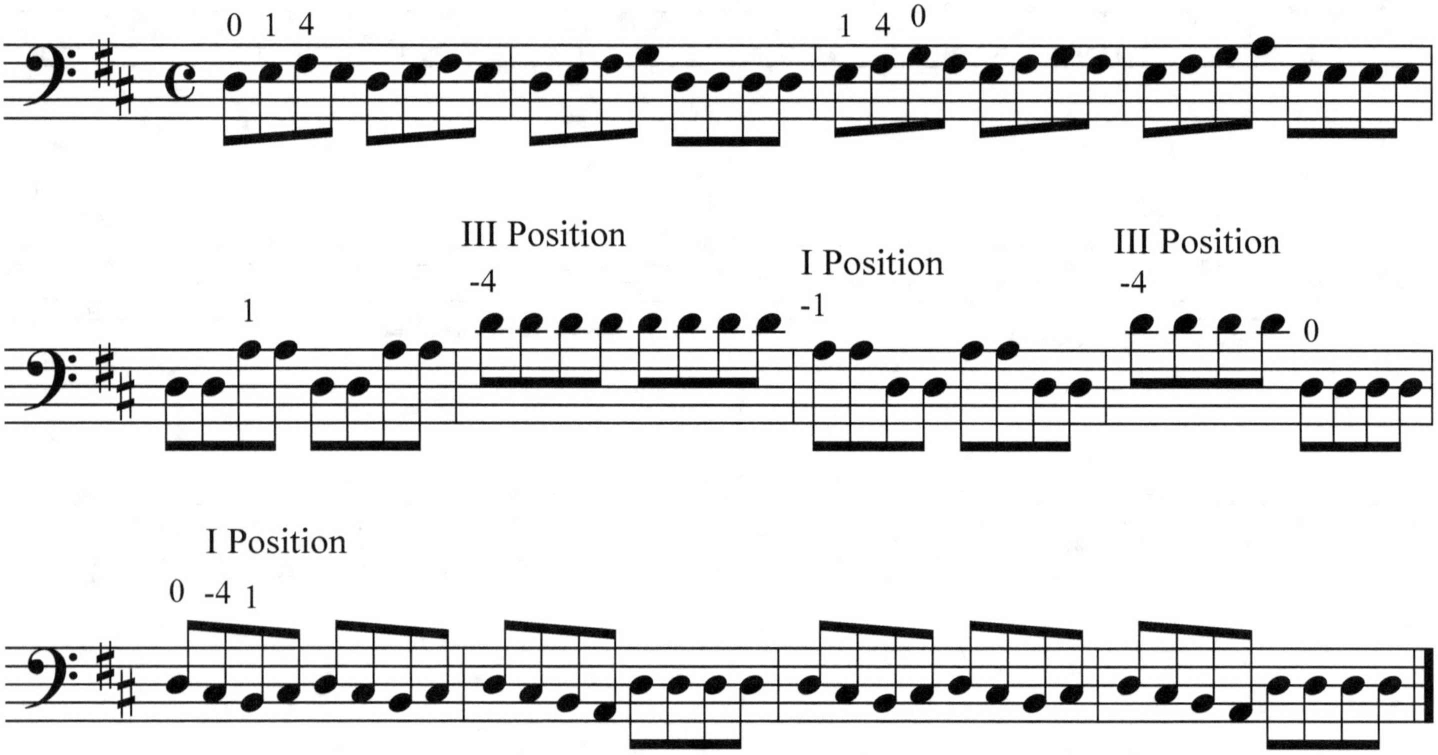

14. Slow Bows: Each note gets 3 counts!

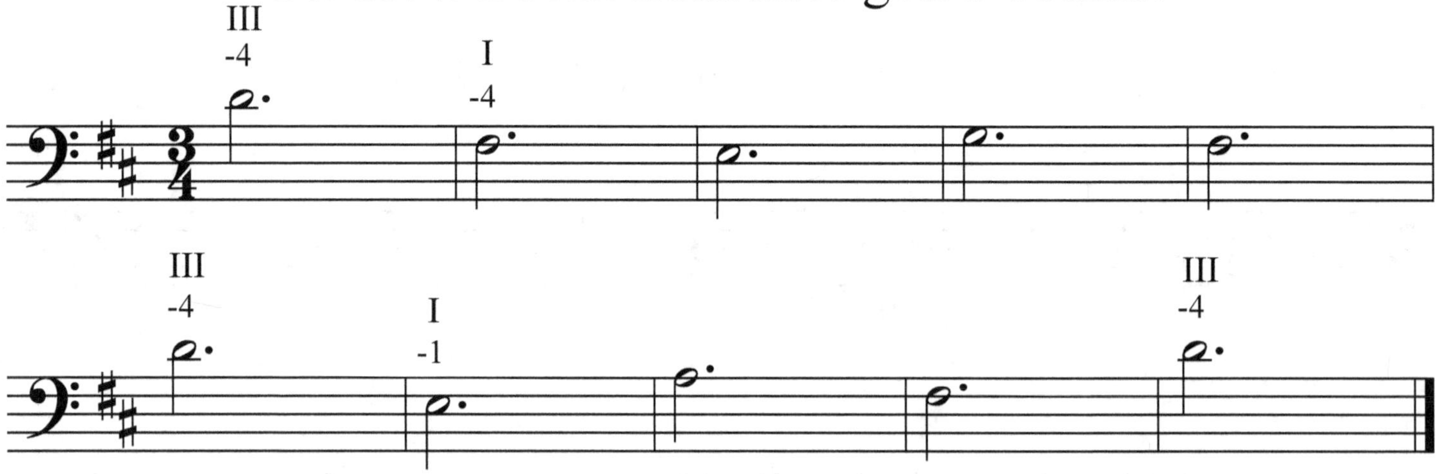

15. Slow Bows: Each note gets 4 counts!

18. Note Practice while Violins Learn the E string

19. Practicing while the Violins play the A Major Scale

©2016 C. Harvey Publications All Rights Reserved.

20. The Minstrel Boy

21. A Minuet by Bach for Violins and Basses

22. The Minstrel Boy for Violas, Cellos, and Basses

23. A Minuet by Bach for Violas and Cellos

This page left blank to eliminate page turns.

24. (Violins Learn Fourth Finger)

25. String Crossing Practice for Telemann

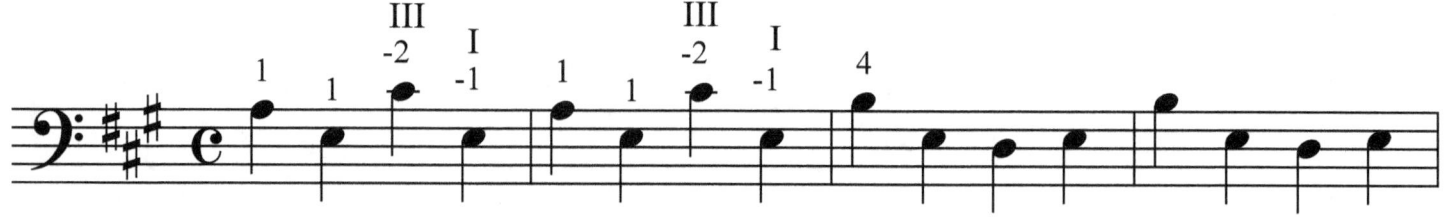

26. Telemann Allegro from Solo #7

27. Telemann Allegro from Solo #7 for Violas and Cellos

28. The Skipping Workout

29. Hornpipe

30. Lady George Murray's Reel

31. Exercise with E

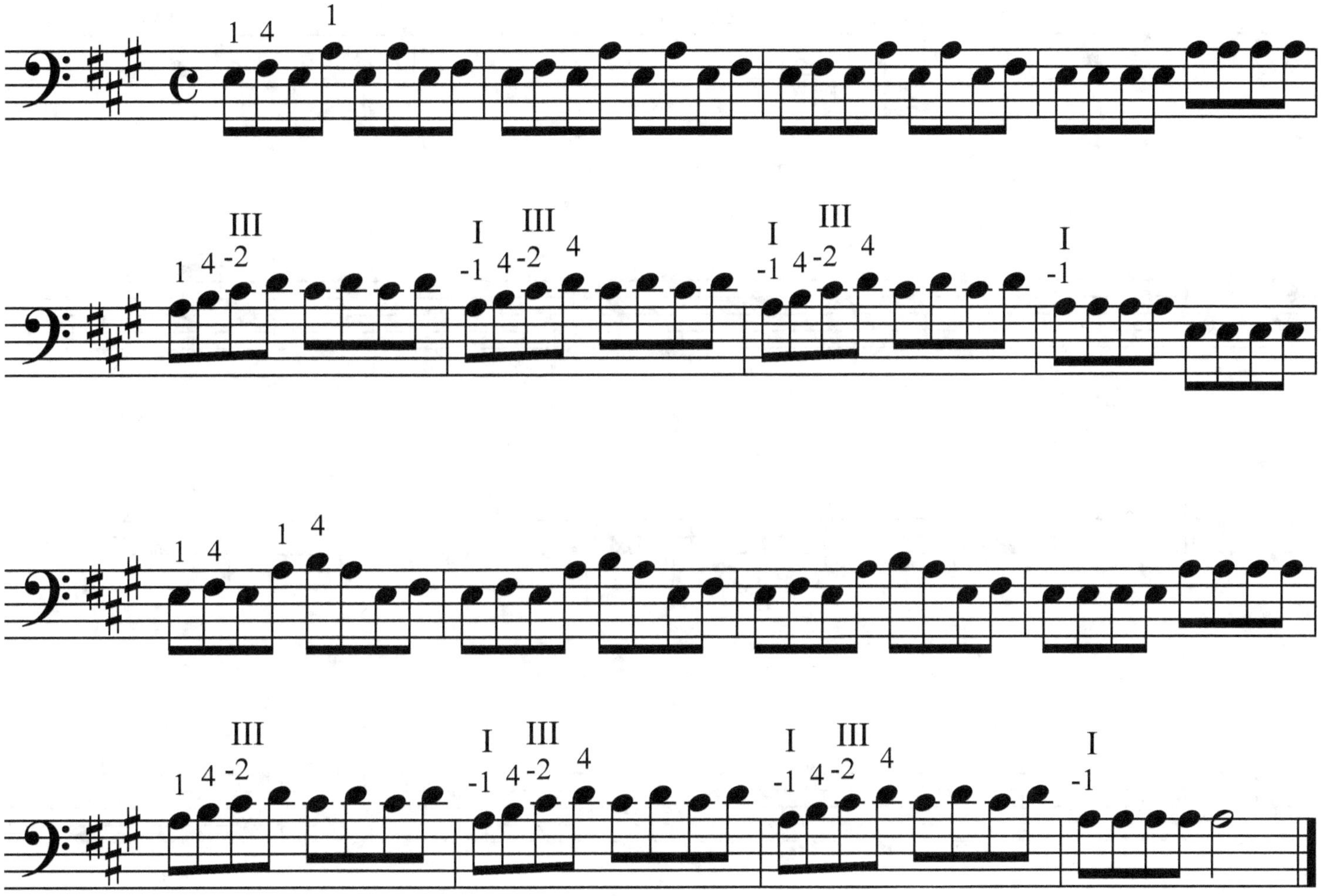

32. Exercise with D

33. Minuet on "Duncan Grey" for Violins and Basses

Advanced Variation for Violins

34. Minuet on "Duncan Grey" for Violas and Cellos

Advanced Variation for Violas, Cellos, Basses

35. Skipping Fingers on D, A, and with E

36. British White Feathers

37. Fiddle Exercise

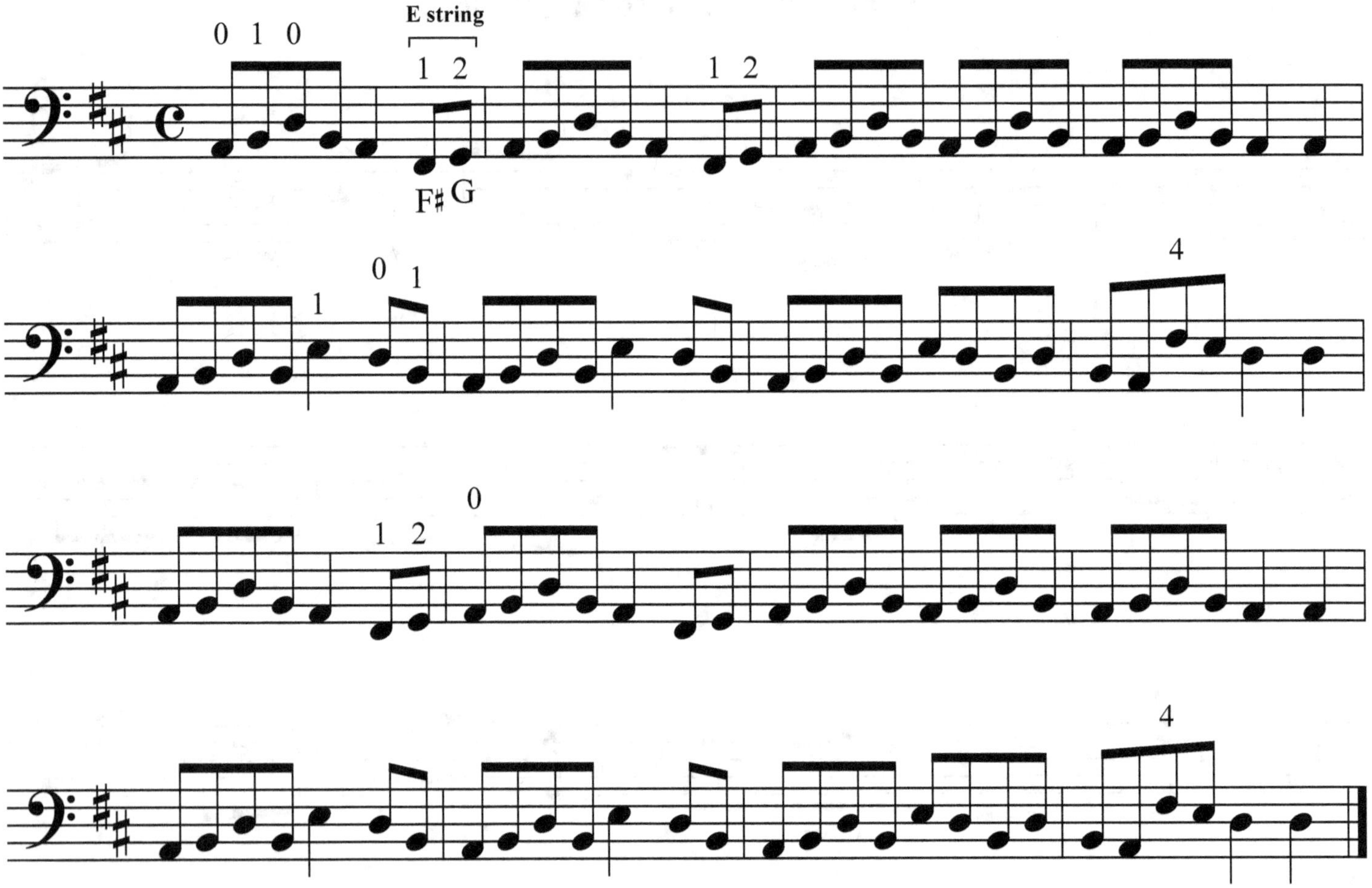

38. Violins Train on the E String

39. Over the River and Through the Woods

Playing the Bass, Book One

40. Captain Oakus

©2016 C. Harvey Publications All Rights Reserved.

41. 2nd Finger "G" and 2nd Finger "C♮"

42. A Menuett by Leopold Mozart

43. A Menuett by J. S. Bach

44. British White Feathers Using Low G and 2nd Finger C

45. Rameau's *Tambourin*

30

46. We Wish You a Merry Christmas

47. Shalom Chaverim

©2016 C. Harvey Publications All Rights Reserved.

(Only basses play: practice shifting to C natural.)

48. Happy Birthday

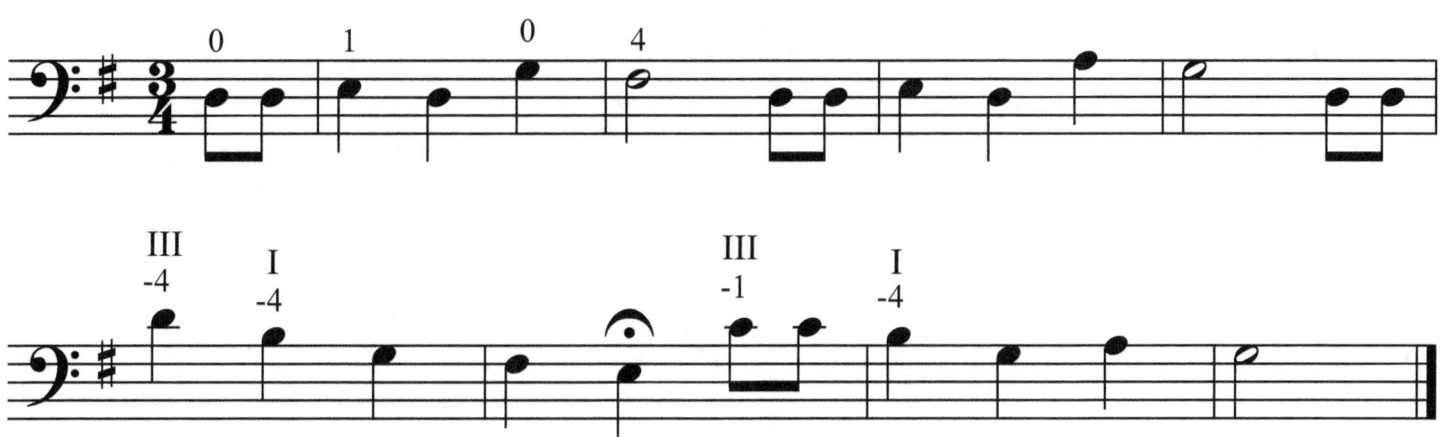

49. Happy Birthday Variation

This page left blank to
eliminate page turns.

50. 2nd Fingers C♮ and F♮

51. C Scale Exercise

52. Skye Boat Song

53. Red Red Rose

Arranged Myanna Harvey

54. Such a Parcel of Rogues!

55. The Snake Charmer's Dance for Cellos and Violas

Interlude

56. The Snake Charmer's Dance for Violins and Basses

57. Bonaparte's Retreat

www.ingramcontent.com/pod-product-compliance
Lightning Source LLC
Chambersburg PA
CBHW051428070526
44584CB00023B/3624